That Time I Got Reincarnated as a SLIME

5

Sho Okagiri Original Story: FUSE Character Design: Mitz Vah

The Story So Far

As Framea continues her travel guide research, she finds herself short on money. Fortunately, it's Rimuru to the rescue with his newest invention—a card you can use in place of cash! But as she indulges in avant-garde desserts and fancy clothing, Framea soon runs up the bill to eye-watering levels! Rimuru said she could use it to her heart's content, but this is going too far—and even worse, the two biggest troublemakers in Tempest are about to add fuel to the fire...

Contents

Chapter 25 Easy-Street Noble Life☆Three Stars!! — 3

Chapter 26 Secret Society☆Three Stars!! — 33

Chapter 27 Clandestine Wining & Dining☆Three Stars!! — 61

Chapter 28 Special Envoys☆Three Stars!! — 91

Chapter 29 Underground Arena☆Three Stars!! — 115

CHAPTER 25

EASY-STREET NOBLE LIFE☆ THREE STARS!!

HAA...

ALL RIGHT...
AND THAT'S WHY YOU HAD THAT ENORMOUS SWAG BAG ON YOU?

I SPENT SO MUCH WITHOUT EVEN THINKING...

HOW CAN I EVER FACE RIMURU-SAMA NOW...?
UGH...

KWA-HA-HA-HA
WHY, WHAT IS EVEN THE PROBLEM!?
HE TOLD YOU TO "EXPERIMENT"! TO "USE IT FOR YOUR GUIDEBOOK WORK"!
YEAH, MY MASTER IS RIGHT!
BESIDES, IT'S NOT LIKE HUMAN NOBILITY WOULD CARE ABOUT THAT KID STUFF!
NOBILITY ...

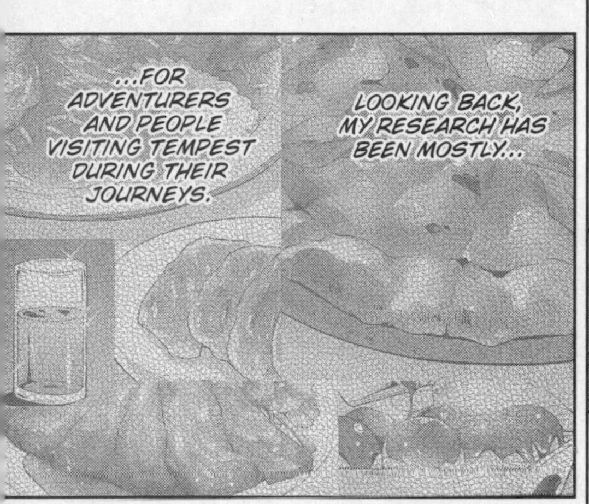
LOOKING BACK, MY RESEARCH HAS BEEN MOSTLY...
...FOR ADVENTURERS AND PEOPLE VISITING TEMPEST DURING THEIR JOURNEYS.

OHH...

BUT I HAVEN'T TARGETED THE ARISTOCRACY MUCH...

RAMIRIS-SAMA! VELDORA-SAMA!
WHAT SAGE ADVICE THAT IS...!

I CAN'T ONLY FOCUS ON COMMON FOLK.
I NEED TO DO GUIDEBOOK RESEARCH FOR NOBLEMEN AND WOMEN TOO, RIGHT?
OOH, BUT...
I DON'T KNOW WHAT THAT SHOULD BE, EXACTLY. WHAT DO YOU THINK I COULD EXPLORE...?
KEH HA HA!

LEAVE EVERYTHING TO ME, RABBITFOLK GIRL!
YEAH! AND ME TOO!

OKAY!

IS...
IS THIS A CASTLE ...?

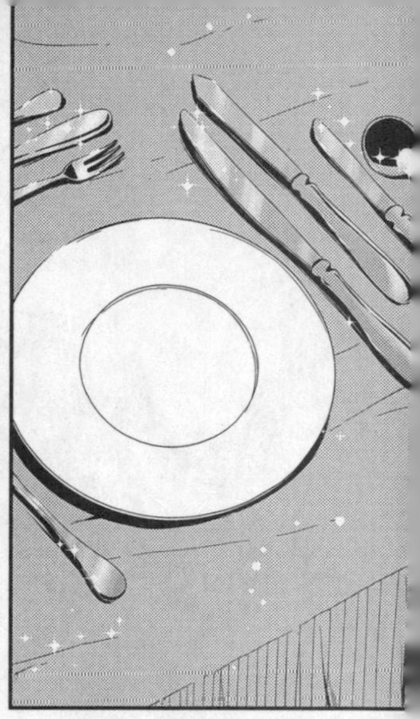

WHAT'S WITH ALL THIS CUTLERY?
IN CASE I DROP ONE, OR WHAT...?

THANK YOU FOR RESERVING OUR WHOLE ESTABLISHMENT TODAY, MY LADY.
WE HAVE PREPARED NOTHING BUT TOP-SHELF ITEMS FOR YOU. I HOPE YOU WILL ENJOY THEM.

T—
TOP-SHELF ...?

WE RE-SERVED THE WHOLE THING !?
WHY HOLD BACK?

IN FACT, I RESERVED EVERY RESTAURANT IN THIS AREA FOR TODAY IN YOUR NAME, FRAMEA.

A...
ALL OF THEM ...?

WHAAAAT!?
ガタッ
GATA (CLATTER)
MM-HMM!
SO START BRINGING ON THE COURSES!

ガク
GAKU (SHIVER)
ガク
GAKU
IS THIS *REALLY* ALL RIGHT ...?

WHAT'RE YOU TALKIN' ABOUT?
GOSO (RUSTLE)
ごそ
GOSO
ごそ
THAT'S WHAT THAT CARD IS FOR!
IT'S HOW YOU'RE SUPPOSED TO USE IT!
HE SAID I COULD USE THIS CARD TO MY HEART'S CONTENT FOR MY WORK AND SUCH...
...AND THIS IS PART OF MY "WORK," RIGHT...?
TO BEGIN, MA'AM...

BOY, AM I STUFFED!
ALL THAT FRESH FRUIT WAS SIMPLY AMAZING!
PON (PAT) ぽん
PON ぽん
HMM...
I WONDER ABOUT THE LACK OF YAKISOBA AND TAKOYAKI, HOWEVER...

YEAH, I GUESS IT WAS PRETTY GOOD...?
BUT I WAS REALLY TOO NERVOUS TO ENJOY IT.
ぽすっ
POSU (PAFF)

SO, WHERE TO NEXT?
YOU WANT TO KEEP GOING?
HEY, WE GOTTA MAKE USE OF THIS CHANCE!
YOU BOUGHT SOME CLOTHES, RIGHT, FRAMEA?
UM, YES.
I SPENT THREE WHOLE GOLD COINS ON THEM, IN FACT.

OH, COME ON! WHAT AN AMATEUR!
LEMME SHOW YOU WHAT THE NOBILITY REALLY WEARS!
ビクッ!
BIKU (TWITCH)
ズビッ!
ZUBI (FWING)
O-OKAY!

...I HAVE NOTHING BUT BUTTERFLIES ABOUT THIS!

LEAVE EVERY-THING TO US.
ぽん
PON

KWAAH HA HA HA!
...IS THIS REALLY OKAY?

WASSHOI (HEAVE-HO)
WASSHOI
OOH! WAS THERE A FESTIVAL OR SOMETHING TODAY?
I DIDN'T HEAR ANYTHING ABOUT IT.
LET'S GO HAVE A LOOK!
WAAH-A-HA-HA!

WASSHOI
WASSHOI
YUSA
THIS SWAYS A LOT, HUH?
YUSA (SWAY)
YES, DOESN'T IT FEEL JUST MAR-VELOUS!?
I AM SURE YOU'D AGREE, FRAMEA!
BURU
AH, UM...
BURU

WHAT IS EVEN GOING ON HERE!?
LOOKING AT IT AGAIN, BOY OH BOY...
NO DOUBT ABOUT IT—THREE STARS, AM I RIGHT?
IS THIS A DRESS OR A EHICLE!?

BUT THE NOBILITY IS ALL ABOUT HOLDING PARADES!
I SAW IT IN RIMURU'S "MANGA" BOOKS!
YES, I READ HIS HOLY TOMES AS WELL.
TRULY, THEY ARE A FONT OF FASCINATING WISDOM.

BUT, UM...
THIS SEEMS MORE LIKE A COSTUME EXHIBITION THAN A NOBLE PARADE...

OH, NOT TO WORRY.
WE THOUGHT OF EVERYTHING. AND IN THOSE BOOKS, WE ALSO LEARNED THIS...

GO AHEAD. TAKE IT, YOU IGNORANT MASSES!
ジャラッ
JARA (JINGLE)
パラ
PARA (SPRINKLE)
WH...
WHAAAA —!?

OOOOO (CHEER)
WELL DONE, MASTER!
IT'S JUST AS THAT BOOK SHOWED!
KWAH-HA-HA-HA!
MOM, WHO'S THAT?
AH... HA-HA...
GAAAN (SHOCK)
NO! YOU MUSTN'T LAY EYES UPON HER!

OOOO
WHAT... WHAT AM I...?
WHAT WILL I EVEN DO ABOUT THIS!?

IF THERE'S ANYTHING YOU NEED, MADAM, PLEASE INFORM US AT ONCE.
THANK YOU AGAIN FOR RESERVING THE ENTIRE ESTABLISHMENT.
PATAN (SHUT)
パタン

IT'S SO BIG...

OOH!
SO SOFT!
OOF!
SO FLUFFY...
ぼすっ
BOSU (BOFF)

I'M...
...SO EXHAUSTED...

HAA...
I HAD NO IDEA LIVING LIKE A NOBLE WAS SO DEMANDING...
I CAN'T GET OVER HOW QUIET IT IS...
BUT THEN, WE DID RESERVE THE WHOLE PLACE.
IT'S LIKE A NIGHT IN A TRANQUIL FOREST.
I THINK I KIND OF LIKE IT.

THIS SILENCE IS NICE AND ALL, YES...
...BUT WHY DO WE NEED IT ALL TO OURSELVES?

OH, BUT...

...WHAT ARE VELDORA-SAMA AND RAMIRIS-SAMA DOING RIGHT NOW?

I'LL LOOK FOR THEM LATER.
......
IS IT REALLY OKAY TO USE IT FOR THIS KINDA THING?
I'M NOT SURE, RIMURU-SAMA...

OF COURSE IT'S NOT.

NO, I...
I'D IMAGINE NOT...

I DEEPLY APOLOGIZE FOR THIS!
SO HERE'S THE STATEMENT FOR ALL YOUR PURCHASES.

ガク
GAKU (QUAKE)
ガク
GAKU
ONE, TEN, A HUNDRED... SO MANY...
HOW MANY GOLD COINS IS THIS...?

HAA...
SO WHAT DROVE YOU TO USE IT LIKE THIS...

...YOU GUYS?
ビク
BIKU (TWITCH)

WE WERE MERELY HELPING HER WITH RESEARCH INTO THE ARISTOC-RACY!
YEAH!
JUST HELPIN' HER WITH THE GUIDEBOOK AND ALL!
DID YOU HAVE TO RESERVE ENTIRE PLACES?
SA (ZWIP)

UGH...
NO SNACKS FOR A WHILE... BOTH OF YOU.

NOW, FRAMEA...
Y—
YES!

IT IS PARTLY MY FAULT FOR NOT DEFINING A CREDIT LIMIT...
...BUT BE MORE CAREFUL NEXT TIME, OKAY?
AND ONE WORD OF ADVICE ...
B-BUT ...!

...YOU'RE BETTER OFF NOT BELIEVING ANYTHING VELDORA AND RAMIRIS TELL YOU.

ALL RIGHT!
HEY!
FRAMEA !?
WHAT DOES THAT MEAN, RIMURU !?
CHAPTER 25☆END

WASSHOI
(HEAVE-HO)
WASSHOI

That Time I Got Reincarnated as a SLIME

The Ways of the Monster Nation

CHAPTER 26
SECRET SOCIETY☆THREE STARS!!
KATSU (CLACK)
KATSU
KATSU
KII (CREAK)
...THE FLOWER?
AT MY BREAST.
YOUR HEART?
EVER BURNING.

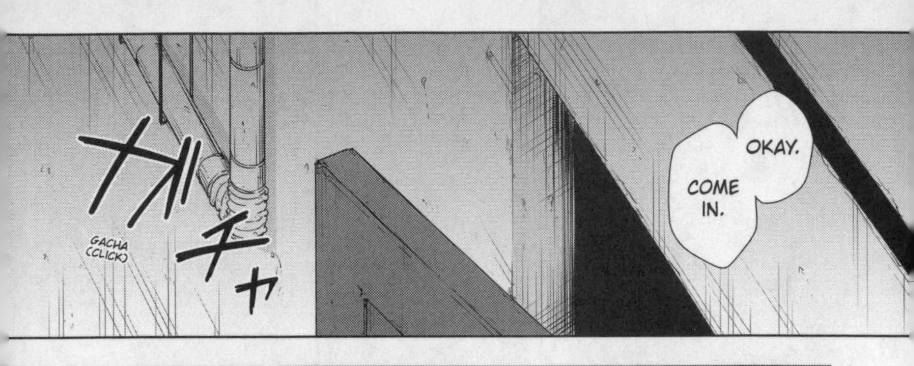
OKAY.
COME IN.
ガチャ
GACHA (CLICK)

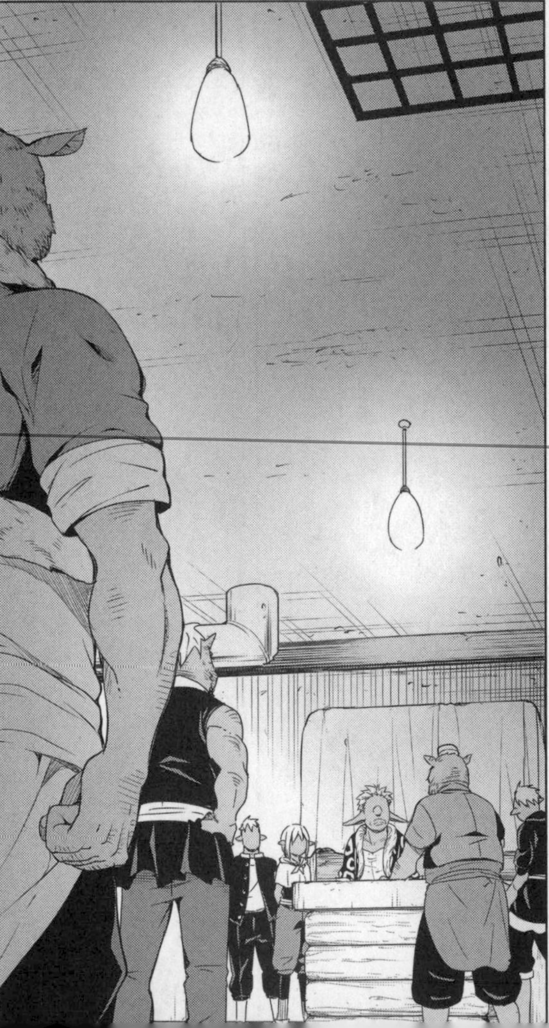

RIGHT. THANK YOU ALL FOR COMING.

TIME TO KICK OFF...
...OUR SOCIETY'S 112TH MEETING.

I'VE CALLED FOR THIS MEETING ...
BASA (FWIFF)
...BE-CAUSE WE'VE FINALLY GOTTEN OUR HANDS ON THESE!

WOW...
WHOA...!

SO I CALLED YOU HERE TODAY...
...BECAUSE I FEAR THERE'S A CHANCE YOUR PHOTOGRAPHS" ARE GETTING LEAKED, FRAMEA.
WHAT!?
BUT I DIDN'T...!
WE DON'T KNOW ALL OF THE DETAILS YET, MIND YOU.
BUT THAT PHOTO TECH IS STILL DANGER-OUS.
IT COULD BE APPLIED TO ALL KINDS OF DIFFERENT FIELDS. BUT EVEN WORSE THAN THAT...

...WE HAVE A BIGGER PROBLEM T DEAL WITH
THERE'S REPORTEDLY A SECRET SOCIETY MEETING DEEP BELOW THIS CITY.
I'M HAVING SOKA STAKE OUT THE MEETING SITE, BUT...
AN UNDER-GROUND SOCIETY...
...YOU SAY?
RIGHT.

IT'S A FAN CLUB...
...FOR SHUNA AND SHION.

WHAT? A, A FAN...
PARDON?
UGH, DON'T PARROT IT BACK AT ME...
IT'S ALREADY ENOUGH OF A HEADACHE.

SO, UM, HOW TO PUT THIS...?
I WANT TO KEEP TABS ON THIS GROUP, AND FIGURE OUT WHAT THEY'RE DOING...
LET'S ERADIC THEM ONCE
I SAY WE JUST CRUSH THEM.
KOKI (CRACK)
CALM DOWN, PLEASE.

THIS...

THIS IS SO DIVINE...!
I'M GLAD TO BE ALIVE...
THIS...
THIS MAKES ME SO HAPPY...SO HAPPY!
THANK YOU SO MUCH...
THANK YOU SO MUCH...

No doubt about it.
The "photos" seem to have leaked to this group.
...I see.
BUT WHERE FROM?
KOKI (CRACK)
SO WE WILL HAVE TO ANNIHILATE THEM.
HOLD IT, HOLD IT.

IT WASN'T YOU, WAS IT, FRAMEA-SAN...?
N-NO! NOT AT ALL...!
YES, I TOOK THOSE PICTURES...
...BUT THE DEVELOPED PHOTOGRAPHS ARE KEPT UNDER CLOSE WATCH WITH VESTER-SAMA...

...AH!
BUT AS INSTRUCTED, I GAVE RIMURU-SAMA'S PHOTOGRAPHS TO YOU TWO AS WELL...
PIKU (TWITCH)

GOHON (KOFF)
GOHON
......
Rimuru-sama...
I see a few familiar faces in the audience.

ガッツン
GATSUN (CLUNK)
AH, NOTHIN' LIKE SHUNA-CHAN IN A SKIMPIER DRESS!
I NEVER THOUGHT I'D BURN THIS SIGHT INTO MY EYES BEFORE I DIED...!
NOW I'LL HAPPILY ACCEPT DEATH WHENEVER IT COMES...!

BEHOLD SHION-SAMA'S UNINHIBITED COUNTENANCE ...!
SIMPLY SEEING THAT SMILE WITH MY OWN EYES...
I FEEL AS IF I'VE DIED AND GONE TO HEAVEN...

UMM...
THIS IS, AH...
HOW WEAK!
THEY ALL NEED TO LEARN SOME DISCIPLINE...!
I SWEAR...
GUNYARI (SPLORP)
THOSE GUYS...
LIKE, AT THIS POINT, IT ALMOST SEEMS EVIL TO ME...
...OR LIKE WORSHIPPING FALSE IDOLS OR SOMETHING.
AH HA HA...
Rimuru-sama seems a tad... affected.

Ughhh... Okay, Soka, keep observing them.
OKAY.

I'M ON THE JOB.

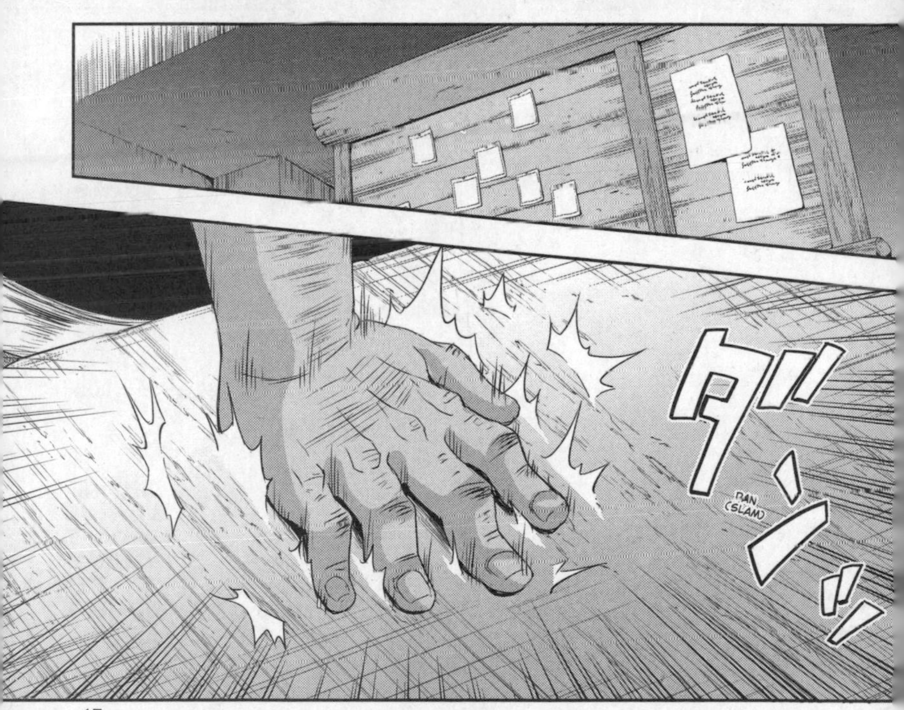
ダンッ
DAN (SLAM)

GOGOGOGOGOGO (RUMBLE)
SHUNA-CHAN IS ALWAYS GOING TO BE NUMBER ONE!
SHE TRULY DESERVES THE TITLE OF "PRINCESS"!
HOW COULD YOU SAY THAT?
SHION-SAMA HAS THE POWER TO EMBRACE AND CONQUER ANYTHING. SHE'D WIN ANY DAY!

TAKE A GOOD LOOK AT THAT BEAMING SMILE.
ARGH! IT'S SO BRIGHT!
NO! LOOK AT THE REFINED, GRACEFUL SMIRK ON SHUNA-CHAN!
MY PICK DESERVES TO BE RIMURU-SAMA'S EMPRESS!!

かあっ
KAAA (BLUSH)
IN THAT CASE, CARRY ON, I SAY!
GUNNYORI (SPLUP)
ぐんにょり…
……
HUH …?

COME ON, BOTH OF YOU.
WE SHOULD DROP THIS...

BA (SPIN)
バッ
WHICH SIDE ARE YOU ON?
EH?
HMM?

THAT'S SUCH AN ENORMOUS QUESTION!
WE DON'T HAVE AN ANSWER!
WELL, HOW WILL WE EVER SOLVE THIS, THEN!?
JUST PICK ONE!

......!
KOKU (NOD)
コクッ
WELL, IF YOU'LL ALLOW ME TO...
...I'LL PICK...

...THE ONLY ONE WHO'LL ALWAYS BE BY RIMURU-SAMA'S SIDE...
DOKIN (BADUM)
ドキン
IT HAS TO BE BENIMARU-SAMA...
KYAAA (SQUEAL)
キャー
KYA
キャッ
KYA
キャッ
PISHI (CRACK)
...Hey, Soka?
YES!

I WOULD LOVE TO HAVE SOEI-SAMA BY MY SIDE...!
SU (ZWIP)
Whoa, whoa, don't go there.
I think it's time we shut this meeting down—
WHAT A HAPPY LITTLE CONVERSATION YOU'RE HAVING.
KO (TAP)
TRULY, IT IS...
...SUCH A WRETCHED ACT.
SHIN (SILENCE)
...

カツッ
KATSU (TAP)
AN ACT...
カツ
KATSU
...I CANNOT SAY I LIKE VERY MUCH.
カツン
KATSU
ガッ
GA (GRAB)
YOU ASK WHO DESERVES RIMURU-SAMA THE MOST...?
ガク
GAKU
ガク
GAKU (SHUDDER)

IT APPEARS YOU REQUIRE SOME EDUCATION.
Whoa, someone stop Diablo!
But who ca—
AAHHHHH!

PHEW...
I WAS PRETTY SCARED FOR A MOMENT THERE...
GOOD THING THE PHOTOS DIDN'T END UP BEING A BIG DEAL.
BUT...

THERE'S ONLY A SELECT FEW PEOPLE IN CONTROL OF THEM.
WHERE COULD THOSE PICTURES HAVE COME FROM?
HA HA HA!
PASHI (SNATCH)
I CAN'T BELIEVE THE MONEY I GOT FOR THOSE LITTLE MAGIC PIECES OF PAPER!
FUAAA (YAWN)
WHAT A TOWN THIS IS...

WONDER IF THERE'S ANY MORE EASY MONEY TO FIND AROUND HERE...?

PURU
PURU (QUIVER)
GOBZO MADE SHION ANGRY TOO, EH?
BUT HE SEEMS KINDA HAPPY ABOUT IT.
SO IT'S GOOD ...?

HAPTER 26☆END

That Time I Got Reìncarnated as a SLIME

The Ways of the Monster Nation

CHAPTER 27
CLANDESTINE WINING & DINING☆THREE STARS!!
LOOKS LIKE WE CAN SEE IT NOW.
GARA
GARA
GARA (RATTLE)
THE MONSTER-LED NATION EVERYONE'S TALKING ABOUT...
HMM...

カラ
KARA
カラ
KARA (RATTLE)

BY THE LOOKS OF THIS HIGHWAY, THE STORIES ABOUT THEIR ADVANCED TECHNOLOGY ARE TRUE, EH?
YES, THIS REGION WILL CERTAINLY GROW, NO DOUBT.
AND IF IT WINDS UP BECOMING A TRANSPORT HUB...

YES.
THAT'S WHY WE CAN'T LET THIS GO BY.

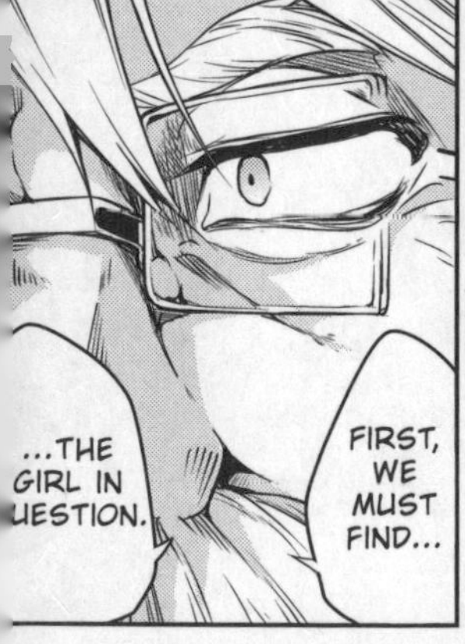
FIRST, WE MUST FIND...
...THE GIRL IN UESTION.

HA- HA- HA- HA-
AH, THE RUMORED RABBIT-FOLK?
MM-HMM.
THE ONE WHO SUPPOSEDLY SPENDS MONEY LIKE IT'S WATER.
JUDGING BY HER INFLUENCE...
...SHE MUST BE A VERY CLOSE ASSOCIATE TO THIS NATION'S DEMON LORD.
THIS IS A DEMON LORD, MIND.
WE'LL HAVE TO APPROACH HIM THROUGH HIS ENTOURAGE.
...AND THAT'S WHERE WE COME IN, IS IT?

I'M SURE IT'LL BE FUN.
YEAH, I CAN'T WAIT NOW...

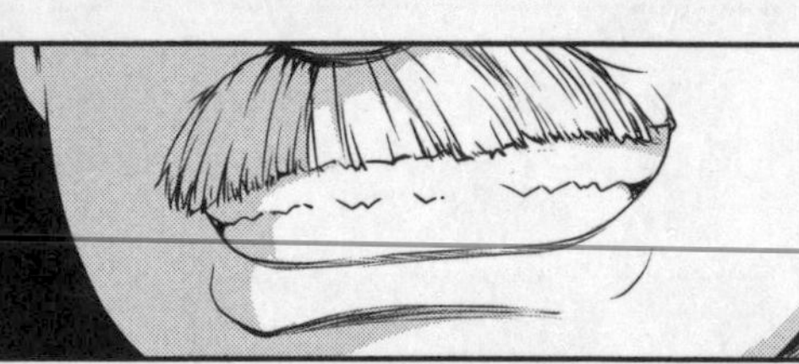

BUT REMEMBER, WE'RE DEALING WITH A NAMED CREATURE HERE.
SO DON'T MESS THIS UP!

OF COURSE WE WON'T.
DOES THAT WRAP UP EVERYTHING WE WERE ASKED FOR?
UMM, LEMME THINK...
EXCUSE US, MADAM.

DO YOU LIVE IN THIS CITY?
Y... YES.
OH, GOOD!
I WAS WONDERING IF YOU COULD TEACH US A LITTLE ABOUT IT.
THAT OUTFIT...
IT MAY NOT LOOK IT AT FIRST, BUT IT MUST HAVE BEEN PRICEY.
THIS MUST BE HER!

SHE DOESN'T SEEM THAT FEARSOME, APPEARANCE-WISE...
WHOA THERE, SIR!

WHO ARE ALL OF YOU?

OH, MY PARDONS!
THAT WAS RUDE OF ME.

WE'RE A GROUP OF MERCHANTS FROM ASSORTED WESTERN NATIONS...
... TRAVEL-ING TO-GETHER.
PLUS, WE ALSO HEARD...
WE HAPPENED TO HEAR OF A RABBITFOLK WHO KNEW A GREAT DEAL ABOUT THIS CITY...
... AND WE THOUGHT SHE MIGHT BE HER.

...THAT SHE HELD AN EXTRAVAGANT PARADE IN TOWN NOT LONG AGO.
!!

OH, THAT, UH...
THAT WAS ME, YES, BUT IT WASN'T THAT FANCY...
UMM...
OH, NO NEED FOR MODESTY!

IT'S THE TALK OF THE TOWN, YET SHE SAYS IT "WASN'T THAT FANCY"!? THIS MUST BE HER...!

SHE SAW THAT WITHOUT EVEN TOUCHING THEM!?
OH, NO, NO!
I'M JUST YOUR AVERAGE MERCHANT, TRULY...
BUT YOU'RE WELL-DRESSED TOO.
YOUR SHOES HAVE ANTI-FATIGUE MAGIC APPLIED...

THIS WOMAN HAS VERY FINE TASTES INDEED! WE HAVE TO STAY VIGILANT!
IT'D TAKE SOMEONE LIKE HER TO BE A DEMON LORD'S CONFIDANT!

SO MIGHT WE BE ABLE TO TALK FOR A LITTLE BIT SOMEWHERE?
I'D LOVE YOUR SUGGESTION FOR A GOOD RESTAURANT OR THE LIKE!
OUR TREAT, OF COURSE!
JIII (GLARE)
じー!!

SUCH A WARY BODYGUARD...! THAT MUST BE HOW IMPORTANT SHE IS!
ARE THEY TRYING TO ASK HER ON A DATE, OR...?

MAYBE NOW'S THE TIME...
...TO TALK ABOUT THE RESEARCH I'M WORKING ON...
AH!
WELL...
IF YOU DON'T MIND ME...

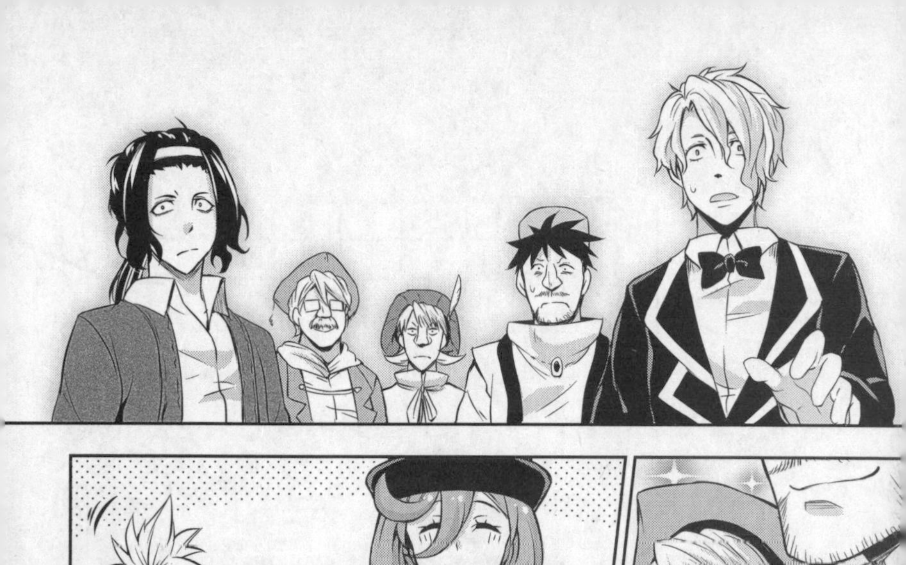

THANKS! THAT'S A BIG HELP!
...YOU SURE ABOUT THIS?

ONCE AGAIN, THANK YOU FOR GRACING US WITH YOUR COMPANY!
UM, IS THIS PLACE ALL RIGHT WITH YOU...?

ARE WE BEING TESTED HERE...!?
IS SHE IMPLYING THIS ISN'T ENOUGH TO SATISFY HER...!?
BOY, I'VE NEVER BEEN IN A JOINT LIKE THIS!
PURU PURU (QUIVER)
NOT HIM TOO!

KOKU (NOD)

DO YOU MIND IF I SIT NEXT TO YOU?
HERE, HAVE A DRINK.
OH, THANK YOU!
TOKU TOKU (GLUK)

YOU SHOULD TRY SOME OF THIS TOO, EVERYONE!

KEEPING AN EYE OUT FOR POISON...?
CERTAINLY. I'D BE GLAD TO.

MM?
WHAT IS THIS!?

IT'S GOOD! AND SO FRAGRANT!

YES, THIS REFINED SAKE IS A NICE LITTLE SPECIALTY OF TEMPEST.

THIS SMOOTH, REFINED TASTE... IT MUST BE FIRST-CLASS! BUT TO HER, IT'S A "NICE LITTLE" DRINK!?

DO YOU DRINK THIS OFTEN, FRAMEA-SAMA?
OH YES!

YEAH, WE WENT THROUGH A WHOLE BARREL A WHILE BACK!
SHE DRINKS SUCH AN ELEGANT BEVERAGE BY THE BARREL!?

WE MAKE SOME DISTILLED LIQUOR TOO, BUT NOT MUCH YET...

ALL THANKS TO THIS FERTILE LAND THEY HAVE...
IT'S NOTHING OUR NATIONS COULD PRODUCE.
WE HAVE TO AT LEAST FORGE A TRADE AGREEMENT...!
GU (CLENCH)

...AH YES, I SEE.
YOU'RE DOING A GREAT DEAL TO SPREAD THE WORD ABOUT THIS CITY'S CULTURE, FRAMEA-SAMA.
I CAN CERTAINLY TELL YOU'RE QUITE THE EXPERT ON THE AREA.

WE'VE ONLY JUST ARRIVED IN TOWN...
...AND ALREADY IT'S A CAVALCADE OF SURPRISES.

OH, IT'S NOTHING THAT SPECIAL...

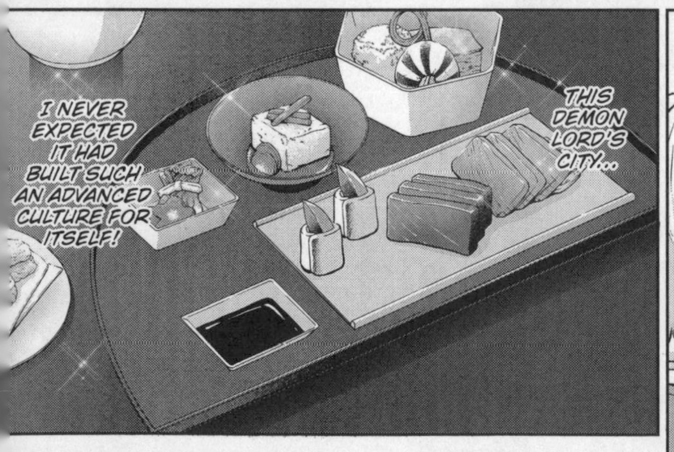
THIS DEMON LORD'S CITY...
I NEVER EXPECTED IT HAD BUILT SUCH AN ADVANCED CULTURE FOR ITSELF!

I MUST DO WHATEVER IT TAKES TO BUILD TRADE TIES WITH MY HOMELAND...
FRESH FISH THIS FAR IN-LAND?
AND TO DO THAT, I'VE SIMPLY GOT...
...TO GET THIS RABBITFOLK ON MY SIDE!
KON (KNOCK)
KON
KOKU (NOD)
KOKU

UM...?
スッ
SU (ZWIP)
HEY, WHOA!
FRAMEA-SAMA...
YES ...?
THOSE FABRICS LOOK QUITE GOOD ON YOU.
I'M SURE A VERY TALENTED TAILOR MADE THAT OUTFIT.
IT BRINGS YOUR BEAUTY TO THE FOREFRONT BRILLIANTLY.

OH, YOU'R DEFINITELY RIGHT!
THIS FABRIC WAS MADE IN TEMPEST!
I'M SURE IT'D MAKE A FINE SOUVENIR FOR YOU.
YES, YES...
THANK YOU.
AND THAT FINE, SILKEN HAIR...
ARE YOU THE DAUGHTER OF A NOBLE FAMILY, PERHAPS?
OH, NO, UH...

GUIII
(PUUUUSH)
TOO CLOSE.

MOST OF THE MONSTERS HERE WERE BORN IN THE FOREST, Y'KNOW.
BURU (QUIVER)
BURU
WHAT'RE YOU GOIN' ON ABOUT?
THE FOREST ...?
A VERY HEALTHY UPBRING-ING, THEN...

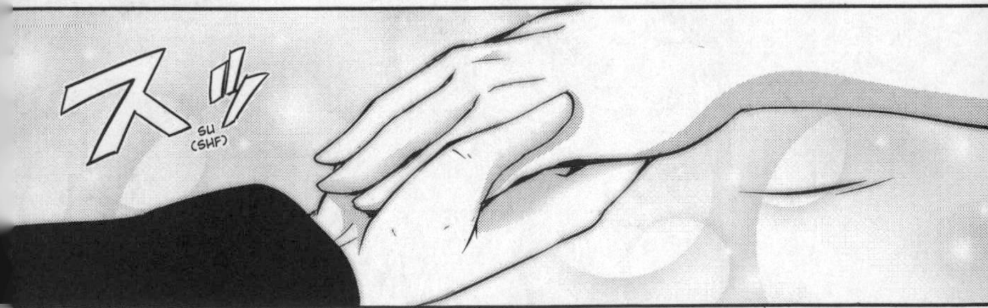
SU
(SHF)

CONSIDERING YOUR CHARMING, KITTEN-LIKE APPEARANCE, YOU HAVE UNIMAGINABLE KNOWLEDGE.
IT IS TRULY ADMIRABLE TO SEE.

I AM BEYOND DELIGHTED TO HAVE MADE YOUR ACQUAINTANCE IN THIS CITY.
DON'T YOU MEAN "RABBIT"?
"KITTEN"? REALLY?

ずーん..
ZUUUN (GLOOM)
SHE'S A FORMIDABLE ONE...

BUT SHE'S A MONSTER. SHE MAY NOT BE ATTRACTED TO HUMAN BEINGS, AND IF NOT...

...I WILL HAVE TO ACT AHEAD OF MY NEIGHBORING NATIONS HERE.

I AM HOPING TO BUILD RELATION-SHIPS WITH THE PEOPLE OF THIS NATION...
...SO I HAVE A SMALL GIFT FOR YOU.
THESE ARE SPICES FROM MY HOMELAND, THE KINGDOM OF MALBARATH.

OH MY!
I COULDN'T
ONE MOMENT, PLEASE!
HERE'S A VERMILION-LACQUER TEACUP FROM BORUSS!

IN THAT CASE...!
ACCEPT THIS FINE SILK FROM THE KINGDOM OF SPIRU!

I-I REALLY APPRECIATE IT, BUT THIS MUCH...?
AHH, IT'S TOO LITTLE TO ELICIT A REACTION. WHAT CAN ATTRACT HER ATTENTION...?
AH!
THAT RING...!

OH, DO PRECIOUS STONES PIQUE YOUR INTEREST !?
GOO (BOOM)

NOT STONES, EXACTLY... BUT THAT'S A "SPECIAL" ITEM, I THOUGHT.
YOU HAVE A VERY GOOD EYE!
THIS IS ONE OF MY FAMILY HEIRLOOMS.
YOU RARELY SEE THIS STONE IN OUR MINES.
I WOULD LOVE YOU TO VISIT MY LAND AND SEE MORE EXAMPLES, FRAMEA-SAMA!

GASHI (GRAB)
W-WAI JUST MINUTE
Y-YEAH!
WE HAVE "SPECIAL" ITEMS IN OUR LANDS TOO...!
VICTORY IS MINE..
THAT'S NEAT 'N' ALL...
...BUT WE GOT LOADSA "RARE" ITEMS IN TEMPEST. "UNIQUES," EVEN.
THIS DAMNED DUMPLING-HEAD...!
HOW THE HELL AM I SUPPOSED TO OFFER HER "UNIQUE" ITEMS!?

^...

HMM
...
OTHER NATIONS, HUH?

THE LAST TIME I WENT ON A TRIP...
...I WAS ADVISED NOT TO STAND OUT.

SO I COULDN'T REALLY WALK OUT IN THE OPEN MUCH.
MAYBE IT'S DIFFERENT NOW...

...YEAH.

I'D CERTAINLY LIKE TO SPEND A WHILE IN ALL YOUR NATIONS, THOUGH.

WH-
WHAAAAAAA!?

WHOA, YOU WOULD ...?

CHAPTER 27☆END

That Time I Got Reincarnated as a SLIME

The Ways of the Monster Nation

CHAPTER 28
SPECIAL ENVOYS☆THREE STAR
OH WOW...
ANOTHER SUPER-CLASSY PLACE...
GOKU (GULP)
ゴク...

I'M QUITE DELIGHTED TO BE GRANTED THE OPPORTUNITY ONCE AGAIN!
W-WELL, THANK YOU VERY MUCH FOR COMING!
OH, THE PLEASURE'S ALL OURS!
IT SOUNDS LIKE YOU AND FRAMEA ARE GETTING ALONG WELL.
I'M HER BOSS. CALL ME...
...SATORU...
LEASE.

THIS IS HER BOSS...
YOU...
KOHON (KOFF)
コホン
SHE LOOKS LIKE A NORMAL GIRL TO ME...

BUT I'VE GOT THE RABBITFO IN MY HAN NOW IT'S T TO CHAR THIS GIR TOO...
I'VE GOT TO TAKE ADVANTAGE OF THIS NATION OF MONSTERS! MY COUNTRY NEEDS ME!
WE CAN'T GO HOME EMPTY-HANDED!
コク
KOKU (NOD)

AHA...
THESE ARE THE GUYS WHO TRIED TO WOO FRAMEA?

I WAS EXPECTING EVIL VILLAINS, BUT THEY ALL SEEM SURPRISINGLY NORMAL.

...IN FACT, I CAN EASILY TELL HOW WEIRDLY NERVOUS THEY ARE.

MJÖLLMILE IS MILES MORE VILLAINOUS THAN THIS GROUP...OH, UH, NEVER MIND!
ALL THE SAME, THOUGH, THIS IS KIND OF EXCITING!
IT REMINDS ME OF SOME OF MY PAST MEMORIES!

WELL, "BOSS" IS ONE WAY TO PUT IT, BUT IN FACT—
MMPH!
SHUBA (SWSSH)

LET'S KEEP THAT UNDER OUR HATS FOR NOW.
I WANT TO FEEL THEM OUT.
OKAY ...?
SHHH!

WELL, HERE'S TO THIS WONDERFUL NEW ENCOUNTER!

I WASN'T SURE WHAT TO EXPECT FROM FRAMEA-SAMA'S SUPERVISOR...
GUI (PUSH)
...BUT I DIDN'T ANTICIPATE SUCH A BEAUTIFUL YOUNG LADY!

UM... YEAH.
WELL, IT'S A MONSTER NATION, SO DON'T READ TOO MUCH INTO THAT...

MAN! TALK ABOUT PUSHY!

AND HIM TOO!
THEY MUST'VE CHARMED FRAMEA INTO LIKING THEM ALL!

SIMPLY SHARING THE SAME SPACE AS YOU RIGHT NOW...
...MAKES THIS TOP-SHELF DRINK ALL THE MORE REFRESHING.
GIVE ME A BREAK...
CARE TO SPEND SOME TIME ELSEWHERE LATER, PERHAPS?

HMM...
SHE'S JUST AS UNREACTIVE TO ROMANTIC ADVANCES AS THE RABBITFOLK. SO...
I MUST SAY...
THIS CITY IS JUST FULL OF SURPRISES.
IT'S AS FINE AS THE CAPITAL OF ENGLESIA...
...OR SHOULD I SAY, EVEN MORE AMAZING IN PLACES!?
AH—
ぱ
PAAA (BEAM)
OHO!
I'M GLAD YOU GET THAT!
ガタッ
GATA (CLATTER)
YES! OH YES!
I FEEL THIS IS TRULY A MAGNIFICENT NATION...!

EVERYTHING FRAMEA-SAMA TOLD US HAS BEEN SO AMAZING!
AND ALL THE STRANGE AND FANTASTIC SIGHTS ARE A WONDER TO SEE!
KOKU (NOD)
AND NOW WE'VE BEEN BLESSED WITH THE REMARKABLE GOOD FORTUNE...
...TO CONFER WITH THE VERY PEOPLE INVOLVED WITH BUILDING THIS LAND!
GOSO (RUSTLE)
AND SO...
...WE ARRANGED FOR AN EXPRESS COURIER TO DELIVER YOU A GIFT FROM ALL OF US.
KOTO (PLINK)

ARE...ARE THESE BLACK PEARLS!?
Unique skill
DILETTANTE
Appraisal, Measure
EXCELLENTLY SPOTTED!
WE WORKED WITH OUR MERCHANT UNION TO PROVIDE THE BEST EXAMPLES OF WHAT WE HAVE TO OFFER AT THE MOMENT!
SATORU-SAMA, I HOPE THAT WE CAN FOSTER A CLOSER PERSONAL RELATION-SHIP...
ALONG THOSE LINES, WE ARE WILLING TO PROVIDE YOU WITH ANYTHING YOU MAY LIKE!
WE LOOK FORWARD TO YOUR CONSIDER-ATION...!!

"PERSONAL" DO THEY MEA TO BRIBE ME
BUT IF THEY'RE BOWING THEIR HEADS THIS FAST, IS SOME OTHER REASON IN PLAY...?
THAT AIN'T REALLY ENOUGH OF A TRIBUTE FOR A DEMON LORD, IS IT?

ピクッ
PIKU (SHUDDER)
DEMON... LORD?
HEY ...!
YEAH, IT'S KIND OF TRUE...

BURU (SHAKE)
MY LORD, PLEASE FORGIVE OU SENSELESS IGNORANCE!
BURU
WHOA!
EESH...
I HID IT BECAUSE I FIGURED THIS MIGHT HAPPEN, BUT...
ALL RIGHT.
WHY DON'T WE GET DOWN TO BUSINESS?

OUR HOME-LAND OF BORUSS...
...IS A TINY REPUBLIC, A COLLECTION OF EVEN SMALLER KINGDOMS, WITH LITTLE MORE THAN ITS NATURE TO BOAST ABOUT.
IN ORDER TO ENSURE THE SURVIVAL OF A SMALL DOT ON THE MAP LIKE OURS...
...WE REASONED THAT WE MUST FIND SUPPORT FROM A NATION LIKE YOURS...
ONE BOUND TO BECOME A VITAL HUB SERVING A VAST REGION.

WE DIDN'T EXPECT A TOWN IN THE MIDDLE OF THE FOREST OF JURA TO BE SO BOOMING.
EVERYWHERE WE TURN, THERE'S MORE WE WISH TO LEARN ABOUT...

THE KINGDOM OF MORAPHA ALSO REQUESTS ASSISTANCE!
WE WILL DO WHATEVER WE CAN FOR YOU ...!

OUR NATION MAY BE SMALL, BUT IT IS STILL OUR HOME.
AND WE ARE ALL WILLING TO LAY DOWN OUR LIVES FOR IT...!

I THOUGHT THESE WERE UNSCRUPULOUS MERCHANTS, BUT THEY'RE SOMETHING MORE LIKE EMISSARIES?
YOUR NATION ...

BUT...

...DID YOU THINK IT'D BE THAT EASY TO GET ON OUR GOOD SIDES?
YOU TOOK A PRETTY CRUDE APPROACH.
NO...
NO!
NOT IN THE LEAST...!
WHAT !?
I'M SORRY, FRAMEA...
...BUT I THINK YOUR WOULD-BE LOVERS APPROACHED YOU STRICTLY FOR COMMERCIAL REASONS.
THAT'S NOT TRUE!
D-DID IT SEEM LIKE I WAS ACTING THAT WAY!?
NO...? THEN WHY WERE YOU TRYING TO HELP THEM!?

UM....
WELL, THE LAST TIME I WAS IN THEIR REGION, I DIDN'T REALLY HAVE FULL FREEDOM TO TOUR AROUND...
I SEE!
...SO YOU WERE JUST CURIOUS, HUH?

THAT RIGH
GETTING TO LIVE HERE, AND BEFRIENDING LOTS OF HUMANS AS WELL...
IT'S MADE ME WANT TO VISIT OTHER PLACES TOO!
YOU SURE YOU WEREN'T JUST FALLIN' FOR PRETTY BOYS?
FRAMEA-SAMA!
スッ
SU (SHF)
WHEN YOU DO, LET ME JOIN YOU!

HE'S STILL GOIN' ON LIKE THAT? WAIT...
DID HE SERIOUSLY FALL FOR HER, OR WHAT...?
HUUUH !?
HE'S THE TYPE THAT CAN'T TELL A LIE, UNLIKE MYSELF...
IT'S NOT FOR A WHILE YET, BUT PERHAPS YOU'D LIKE TO COME SEE OUR HARVEST FESTIVAL!
OH, I HEARD ABOUT THAT! AN EVENING FEAST, WHERE EVERYONE'S SURROUNDED BY FLOWERS THAT BLOOM AT NIGHT...

...GUESS THERE'S NO ULTERIOR MOTIVE, THEN.
SO LET'S FORGET ABOUT PERSONAL RELATIONSHIPS OR QUICK RESULTS.
FIRST, LET'S LEARN MORE ABOUT EACH OTHER...AS PEOPLE AND AS MONSTERS.
BI (BWIP)
THE NATION-LEVEL TALKS CAN WAIT UNTIL AFTER THAT.
HOW'S THAT SOUND?
YOU ARE TRULY A GENEROUS LEADER!
THANK YOU FOR YOUR CONSIDERATION!

AN EVENING FLOWER FESTIVAL, HUH?
I'D LIKE TO ATTEND TOO.
MOGU (MUNCH)
もぐ
もぐ
MOGU

YES, AND THE CITY GIRLS HAVE SPECIAL OUTFITS THEY WEAR FOR THE OCCASION.
IT'S QUITE A GAUDY EVENT, I THINK YOU'LL FIND!

THOUGH I MUST SAY, IN RECENT YEARS...
...THEIR WARDROBE HAS TENDED TOWARD THE, AH, MORE DARING.
OHO?
ピク
PIKU (PRICK)

TELL ME MORE.
UM...?

HELLO.
HERE ARE TODAY'S DOCUMENTS, RIMURU-SAMA...
...OH?
HIRA (FWP)

AHH, WE SHOT THAT AT THE CLUB LATER!!
PASHA (SNAP)
PASHA
WHAT IS THIS...?

GOGOGO (RUMBLE)
GOGO
Y-YES, UM, I WAS MEETING WITH SOME MERCHANTS FROM THE WEST, AND...
BIRI (RIP)
EEP!

...AND SO, MY ALLOWANCE WAS REDUCED.
CHAPTER 28☆END

That Time I Got Reincarnated as a SLIME

The Ways of the Monster Nation

WAAAAAA
(CHEER)
ワァァァァァァァ
ド
DO
(THUD)
ARRGH
...!
グラ
GURA
(STAGGER)
HEH
...

HAPTER 29
NDERGROUND ARENA☆
HREE STARS!!
KWAAAH HA HA HA HA!!
Another instant KO! Such over-whelming strength!
The winner, once again, is the mysterious "Dragon Mask"!
OOOOO (ROAR)

I HEARD RUMORS ABOUT A HIDDEN ARENA UNDERNEATH THE OFFICIAL ONE...
...AND IT REALLY DOES EXIST!
IT'S S INTENS ...!
BUT ...

THAT MASKED WARRIOR SEEMS FAMILIAR...

......

...NO. WHAT WOULD HE EVER BE DOING HERE...?

A FEW WEEKS AGO...
DO I HAVE TO CHECK THIS EXPERIMENT AGAIN...?
IT'S SO BORING.
RAMIRIS, CAN YOU HANDLE THAT FOR ME?
FIGURE OUT A WAY TO DO IT YOURSELF!
Y HANDS ARE FULL TOO!
I'LL BUY YOU AS MANY DESSERTS FROM YOSHIDA-SAN'S PLACE AS YOU WANT.
SO PLEASE?
YOU WILL!?

MASTER! MASTER!
JIII (GLARE)
HMM ...
WELL, WAIT.
HM?
UH... WHAT?
I THINK DEENO'S GOT SOME WEIRD MYSTERY SOURCE OF INCOME!
SOUNDS SUSPICIOUS.
ALL HE DOES IS LIE AROUND, AND HE CAN'T BE GETTING THAT MUCH OF AN ALLOWANCE!
HE'S GOT TO BE UP TO SOMETHING, I TELL YOU!
WHAT? NO! I'VE GOT NOTHING LIKE THAT!
BIKU (SHIVER)

ドカッ
DOKA (WHUMP)
SO...
DEENO...
WH-WHAT, VELDORA?
VELDORA...I HATE DEALING WITH HIM.
I'M NOT DOING ANYTHING WRONG.

GASHI (GRAB)
OH, COME NOW! I JUST WANTED TO CHAT A BIT.
I DIDN'T DO ANY-THING!
ギュウゥ
GYUUU (SQUEEZE)
UGH, ALL THAT DAMN MUSCLE...!

HANG ON. MUSCLE...?

MAYBE I CAN MAKE USE OF THAT...
THE MONEY FROM THE PICTURES IS ALMOST GONE... IT'S TIME FOR A NEW SCHEME.
WELL, ACTUALLY ...
I'VE BEEN MEANING TO DISCUSS SOMETHING WITH YOU.

KWAH-HA-HA-HA!
WAAAAAA (CHEER)
ANYONE WHO WANTS TO CHALLENGE ME, STEP FORWARD!
HYU (FWISH)
SUKON (THWAP)
NRGH!

DAMN IT ALL, DEENO, WHAT ARE YOU...?
PIRA (FLAP)

YOUR PERFORMANCE SUCKS!

And now, our next challenger...
HAAH...
MAN!
YOU GOTTA DO BETTER FOR ME!
WAAAAAAAAAAA
HEY, WHO'RE YOU GONNA BET ON NEXT?
THERE ARE SOME GOOD ODDS ON THE CHALLENGER ...
...BUT HE'S SHOWN NO SIGNS OF LOSING AT ALL.
YEAH...
ALL THESE ORDERS ...

ZA (SHK)
MMM?

SO I REALLY EARN A HUNDRED GOLD COINS IF I WIN, EH!?
Now let the battle... begin!
OH, YOU'RE NEXT?
IF YOU CAN WIN, YES...
DA (DASH)

BACHII (BASSHH)
HNGBH !?
ZUZAZA (SKIIID)
SHIIIN (SILENCE)
A... Another instant victory!!

ピク
PIKU (TWITCH)
ピク
PIKU
He didn't even pose a challenge to him!
WAAAAAAAA (CHEER)
AAH HA HA HA!
HEH...
A... Another instant victory!!
ヒュン
HYUN (FWISH)
トスッ
TOSU (THUNK)
NGH!

STOP INSTA-KILLING!! FIND A WAY TO STRETCH IT OUT!
PIRA (FLAP)
AY, ME!
I-I THINK I MAY BE A TAD FATIGUED, OR THE LIKE... MAYBE!
PERHAPS THE NEXT CHALLENGER STANDS A BETTER CHANCE!
ZAWA (CHATTER)
ZAWA
AH-HA-HA-HA!

THAT HAS TO BE VELDORA SAMA, RIGHT...?
I MEAN... WHAT'S HE EVEN DOING!?

JARARA (JANGLE)
KWAH-HA-HA-HA-HA!

ALL YOUR DETAILED ORDERS DID VEX ME, DEENO...
...BUT LOOK AT HOW MUCH PROFIT THEY BROUGHT US!
I COULDN'T HAVE DONE IT WITHOUT YOUR HELP.
IT NEVER GETS OLD, DON'T YOU AGREE?

YEAH, WORD ABOUT YOU IS STARTING TO GO AROUND...
HEY, I KNOW!
AND HAVING THE CROWDS CHEER FOR ME CERTAINLY DOESN'T FEEL BAD EITHER!
NEXT TIME SOMEONE KINDA STRONG SHOWS UP, HYPE IT UP AND THROW THE MATCH FOR ME.
MM?
ARE YOU SURE YOU WANT ME TO LOSE?
HEY, YOU GOTTA TOS 'EM A CARR SOMETIME
IT'S JUST AN ACT!
HMM ...?
WELL, DEENO, I SUPPOSE I WILL PLAY ALONG...
...THIS TIME.

GAAAAAAH!!
ZAN (SLASH)
I HAVE BEEN BESTED!!

BATA (CRASH)
HUH ...?
He...He's down!
The chal-lenger is victorious!
ZAWA (SHUDDER)
We have our first prize winner ...!

YES, A PERFECT PERFOR-MANCE...
HEH.

NRGH!
DOSU (THWACK)

......
ピラ
PIRA (FLAP)
WHAT? THAT WASN'T GOOD...?
We will now have a brief inter-mission ...

DAMN HIM...
WHAT DOES HE POSSIBLY HAVE TO COMPLAIN ABOUT?
OH...?

THE RABBIT?
HI, UM...
WOULD YOU MIND LETTING ME INTERVIEW YOU FOR A LITTLE BIT?
NOT AT ALL.
THANK YOU VERY MUCH...
...VELDORA-SAMA!

KWAAH HA HA HA!
ASK ME ANYTHING YOU LIKE!

...HM?

HYU (WHISH)
GNHH!
TOSU (THUNK)

THAT'S A SECRET IDENTITY!!

フイッ
FUI (SPIN)
...I AM NOT VELDORA.
NO?
BUT...

NO, I AM NO ONE AS GRAND AND LOFTY AS VELDORA!
VELDORA IS FAR MORE BRILLIANT THAN I!!
HOW CONVINCING...

......

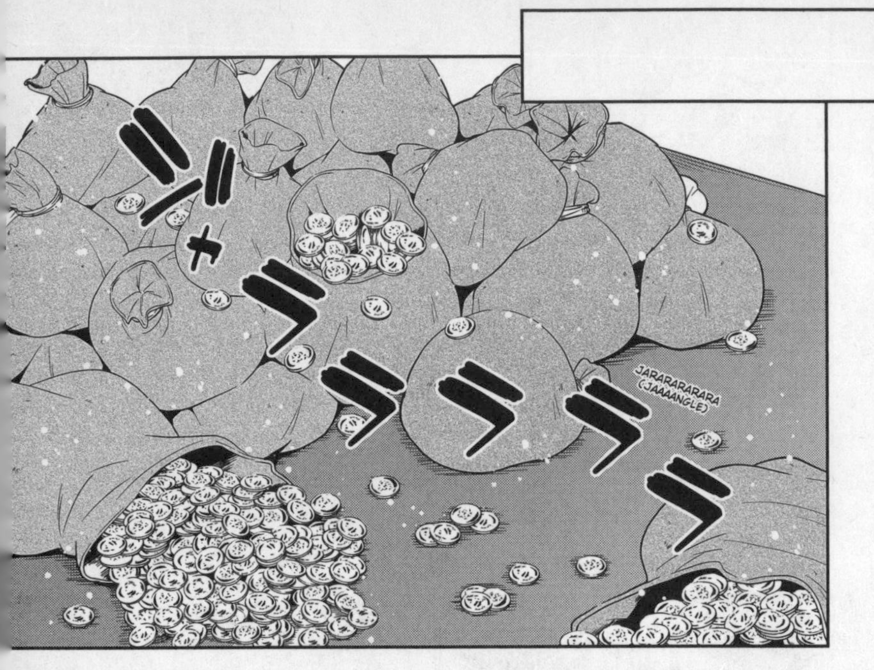
JARARARARARA
(JAAAANGLE)

WE'RE AN INVINCIBLE TEAM, YOU AND ME!
HEH HEH...

HEH-HEH... THAT'S RIGHT, DEENO.
A SINGLE THROWN MATCH, AND LOOK AT HOW MUCH MORE WE EARN...

TRULY, YOU ARE A GENIUS WHEN IT COMES TO THESE THINGS!
バシ
BASHI
OW!
STOP THAT!
バシ
BASHI (SMACK)
バシ
BASHI

ゲホッ
GEHO (KOFF)
...BUT IF WE KEEP THIS UP...
...WE'LL RAKE IN THE CASH SUPER-EASY, SO...

BOY, YOU TWO SURE ARE WORKIN' HARD, HUH?

AH...R-RIMURU-SAN...
AH!
DAMN IT, RAMIRIS! YOU SNITCHED ON US!
HA! NOT LIKE I'M GONNA LET YOU HAVE ALL THE FUN!
SO, HOW ABOUT WE TALK ABOUT THIS A LITTLE?
ガシッ
GASHI (GRAB)

UGH.

OKAY, CAN I HEAR YOUR STORY?
LEMME JUST SAY, I HAVE TESTIMONY...

-Testimonial 1-

-Testimonial 2-

AND SO...
...YOU'RE UNDER SUSPICION OF RUNNING AN UNAUTHORIZED COMBAT LEAGUE AND BETTING ENTERPRISE.
MASTER ...
I'M NOT ASKING YOU TO STOP HOLDING EVENTS...
...BUT IF YOU'RE USING VELDORA FOR THEM, IT'S PRETTY MUCH FRAUD, YOU KNOW?
CRIMINAL

WHAT'S THE PROBLEM WITH IT? IT WAS A BIG HIT.
OH, YOU THINK?

WELL, IF YOU LIKE IT THAT MUCH, I COULD APPOINT YOU HEAD OF ALL OUR ARENA EVENTS...
ガタ
GATA (CLATTER)
WHOA! I DON'T WANNA MAKE MY HOBBY MY JOB!
UGH...
I KNEW I SHOULD'VE STOPPED AT THE PHOTOGRAPHS.

THE PHOTOGRAPHS ...?
OH.

SO THE SWIMSUIT PHOTOS THAT GOT LEAKED...
...WERE YOU BEHIND THOSE, PERHAPS?

N-NO, UH... HUH?
I-I DUNNO WHAT YOU MEAN...

SHUNA, CALL SHION IN HERE.
AT ONCE.
WHOA...!
TIME FOR A SECOND INVESTIGATION.

WE BETTER HAVE SHION PREPARE SOME DINNER FOR YOU...
LOOKS LIKE IT'S GONNA BE A LONG NIGHT.
HOPE YOU'RE READY TO BE PUNISHED.

WAIT A SECOND ...
I, I CAN EXPLAIN ...
NOOOO-OOOO!

CHAPTER 29☆END

OOOOO
(ROAR)

Special Thanks

Creator: Fuse-sensei
Character Design: Mitz Vah-sensei

Taiki Kawakami-sensei
Shiba-sensei
Shizuku Akechi-sensei
Tae Tono-sensei

Aramasa-sama
Uorui-sama
Ezaki-sama
Tetsuro Seki-sama
Fu Yamaguchi-sama
Ibuki Ichinose-sama

All the editors

VOLUME 5!!
CONGRATS, OKAGIRI-SENSEI!
MITZ VAH

THE WAYS OF THE MONSTER NATION
5
CONGRATS ON RELEASING VOLUME 5!!
VELDORA AT HIS PEAK IS SO AWESOME!!
川上泰樹
TAIKI KAWAKAMI

HERE'S TO VOL. 5!

OORAY
OLUME 5☆
FRAMEA-
CHAN♥
あけちしずく
SHIZUKU AKECHI

OKAGIRI-SENSEI, CONGRATULATIONS ON VOLUME 5 OF THE WAYS OF THE MONSTER NATION!
I ALWAYS ENJOY READING ABOUT WHAT KIND OF NONSENSE (!?) FRAMEA GETS UP TO NEXT!
TAE TONO
MY SERIES TRINITY IN TEMPEST IS RUNNING IN WEDNESDAY'S SIRIUS RIGHT NOW!

PRESS "SNOOZE" TO BEGIN.
DEATH MARCH TO THE PARALLEL WORLD RHAPSODY
MANGA
After a long night, programmer Suzuki nods off and finds himself having a surprisingly vivid dream about the RPG he's working on…only thing is, he can't seem to wake up.
LIGHT NOVEL
YEN ON
www.yenpress.com
Death March to the Parallel World Rhapsody (novel) © Hiro Ainana, shri 2014 / KADOKAWA CORPORATION
Death March to the Parallel World Rhapsody (manga) © Ayamegumu 2015 © Hiro Ainana, shri 2015/KADOKAWA CORPORATION

THE CHART-TOPPING SERIES THAT SPAWNED THE EXPLOSIVELY POPULAR ANIME ADAPTATIONS!

SWORD ART ONLINE, VOL. 1-22
LIGHT NOVEL SERIES
SWORD ART ONLINE © REKI KAWAHARA
KADOKAWA CORPORATION ASCII MEDIA WORKS

SWORD ART ONLINE PROGRESSIVE, VOL. 1-6
LIGHT NOVEL SERIES
SWORD ART ONLINE: PROGRESSIVE © REKI KAWAHARA
KADOKAWA CORPORATION ASCII MEDIA WORKS

SWORD ART ONLINE PROGRESSIVE, VOL. 1-7
MANGA SERIES
SWORD ART ONLINE: PROGRESSIVE
© REKI KAWAHARA / KISEKI HIMIIRA
KADOKAWA CORPORATION ASCII MEDIA WORKS

SWORD ART ONLINE, VOL. 1-10
MANGA SERIES
SWORD ART ONLINE: AINCRAD
© REKI KAWAHARA / TAMAKO NAKAMURA
KADOKAWA CORPORATION ASCII MEDIA WORKS

SWORD ART ONLINE: GIRLS' OPS, VOL. 1-7
MANGA SERIES
SWORD ART ONLINE: GIRLS' OPS
© REKI KAWAHARA / NEKO NEKOBYOU
KADOKAWA CORPORATION ASCII MEDIA WORKS

VISIT YENPRESS.COM
TO CHECK OUT ALL THESE TITLES AND MORE!

www.YenPress.com

That Time I Got Reincarnated as a SLIME
The Ways of the Monster Nation

Translation: Kevin Gifford • Lettering: Barri Shrager

Yen Press
150 West 30th Street, 19th Floor
New York, NY 10001

Visit us at yenpress.com
facebook.com/yenpress
twitter.com/yenpress
yenpress.tumblr.com
instagram.com/yenpress

First Yen Press Edition: July 2021

Yen Press is an imprint of Yen Press, LLC.
The Yen Press name and logo are trademarks of Yen Press, LLC.

The publisher is not responsible for websites (or their content) that are not owned by the publisher.

Library of Congress Control Number: 2020936422

ISBNs: 978-1-9753-1363-0 (paperback)
978-1-9753-1362-3 (ebook)

10 9 8 7 6 5 4 3 2 1

BVG

Printed in the United States of America